HOME SERIES

HOME SERIES
STORAGE SPACE

BETA-PLUS

CONTENTS

P. 4-5

This small apartment makes optimal use of the available space: a clever storage solution lies hidden behind every wall. Designed by interior architect Philip Simoen.

P. 6

The library of a couple with a passion for old books and antiques.
The French tripod pedestal table is made of oak and is from the eighteenth century. The candelabrum is from the same period.
The small chair is a nineteenth century Irish piece.

INTRODUCTION

L ess crowded rooms, optimal use of space and less time wasted: well thought out storage space ensures peace of mind and greater efficiency in day to day life. Paradoxically, the challenge is often to make these cumbersome elements invisible by ensuring that they blend into the décor. However, when they are well chosen and well positioned, the aesthetic qualities of additional storage units often more than justify their metres squared.

This volume showcases several projects where cleverly designed and positioned storage spaces have been integrated into both contemporary and old-style interior designs. Whether it be duel-purpose rooms or compact, modular or tailor-made furniture pieces, this book proposes some highly effective space-saving solutions and cunning ways to combine storage and décor elements while still making the most of the available space. All of these attractive, practical and original ideas can be personalised to create an interior design which is well-ordered and organised, and therefore relaxing.

P. 8
The living room-cum-library of Marcel Nies, a major international authority on oriental art.

P. 10-11
This bedroom was created by Stéphanie Laporte. Several storage spaces and a hidden radiator are concealed behind the sycamore cupboard doors and panelling. The white leather foot rest at the bottom of the bed is by Christian Liaigre.

A REFUGE ON THE BELGIAN COAST

Over almost the last fifty years, the company Obumex has developed a solid reputation as a designer and producer of global kitchen, interior and office concepts, from the foundation work right through to the finishing touches.

The simple designs always have a sense of class and elegance about them. This apartment overlooking the sea, designed and created by the architect Tom Sileghem, is no exception.

The design beautifully demonstrates how it is possible to create plenty of storage spaces for a large family while, at the same time, maintaining an open and airy atmosphere.

P. 14-17
A finely brushed and stained oak veneer wall. Ceiling height rotating doors
are used throughout this house to ensure that the storage space blends
invisibly into the décor. The wide oak floorboards have been lightly bleached.

The dining room table was tailor-made by Obumex.

P. 18
The kitchen counter and feature wall
are made of soft natural Giallo Dorato
stone. The top sliding doors are
electric. Tap by Dornbracht.

P. 20-21
By incorporating as many quasi-invisible cupboards as possible and by creating some confined but carefully designed rooms, the designer has successfully optimised the available space.

A LIVING ROOM-CUM-LIBRARY

WITH A REFINED ATMOSPHERE

F or the architect Xavier Donck, the integration of high-quality antiques into an architectural project requires a step away from the ordinary.

His starting point was an eclectic antique vision. The individual character of these pieces is beautifully complemented by the rooms he has created, just as any modern work of art integrates perfectly into a contemporary home.

When developing this feature, Donck worked closely with the antique dealers Alain and Brigitte Garnier. For all of them, it was extremely important to ensure the viability of the space and the furniture and artefacts (mostly from the nineteenth century) contained therein.

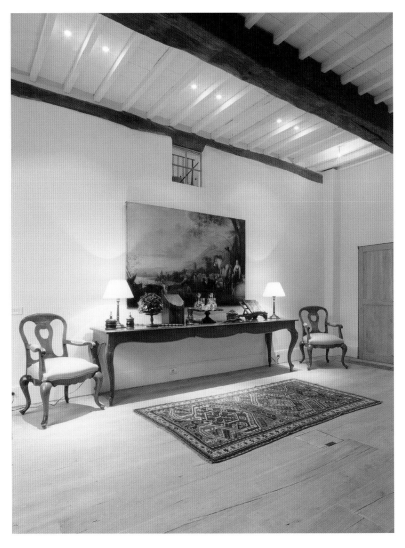

P. 22-23
The panelling with integrated bookcase was designed by the architect Xavier Donck.
The decorations and antiques were provided by Garnier.
The walnut Provencal console table (around 1860) is flanked by two Scandinavian chairs (1820).

A BEAUTIFUL
AND PRACTICAL TOWN HOUSE

This town house, which dates back to the beginning of the twentieth century, has been completely transformed by the architect Christine von der Becke.

The brief was to achieve a balance between an austere design and modern trends regarding space, light, openness and comfort, and at the same time to maximise the amount of storage space.

P. 24-25
In order to open up the space and create more light, the structure of the building had to be modified. The corridor was removed and the landing extended to provide access to the children's bedrooms and the bathroom.
Centre: some examples of large storage cupboards.

P. 26-27
The middle room has been transformed into a walk-in wardrobe and connected to the bedroom to increase the sense of openness. The flow of light creates a warm and homely atmosphere. The wardrobe is made of painted MDF and stained oak. The sliding doors are made of stained oak.

P. 28-29
The kitchen and dining area have been combined and look out over the terrace and garden.
The parquet floor has been partially restored and polished.
The bespoke kitchen cupboards are made of MDF and stained oak. The cupboards around the top of the room provide a discrete storage solution.
Chairs by Ethnicraft, lamp by Constanzia and built-in spotlights by Modular.

THE MASTER ROOMS OF

A RESTORED FORMER *BRASSERIE*

T hese two rooms in a former brasserie have been meticulously restored by their owners (an interior designer and a renowned antique dealer). They epitomise the duo's particular taste for natural eclecticism. Far from being concealed, the storage spaces take pride of place as integral features of the décor.

The couple's approach is perfectly illustrated by the imposing antique bookcase that increases the scale and grandeur of the interior.

Wall bookcase made from parts of an eighteenth century pine portico from Ireland.

A pair of double-faced oak display cabinets are used to store an exceptional collection of antique sketches and miniature portraits.

CALM AND VOLUPTOUS

Once their children had flown the family nest, a couple swapped their home in the suburbs for this city centre apartment designed by Stéphanie Laporte.

For the most part, the layout of the apartment – with the living and dining rooms positioned in the centre – is determined by the concrete structure of the building.

Wood panelled flooring is used throughout most of the apartment. All of the furniture is tailor-made and virtually all of the rooms in the apartment contain a large number of storage units. The many built-in cupboards merge unseen into the walls. These walls are devoid of any decoration, with the exception of a few display cabinets which appear like full length paintings. The lateral planes and unbroken lines create the impression of a neat and immaculate ensemble. Your gaze moves freely around the room. The harmonious combination of materials also accentuates the sense of space.

P. 32 and opposite
The dining room is fitted with tailor-made built-in cupboards on all sides.
The closed cupboards serve as storage space while the display cabinet with
integrated lighting showcases a beautiful collection of antique plates.

The television room
with a writing table.

P. 34-35
The kitchen was designed and produced by Top Mouton.

AN IMAGINARY PAST

F. or the purposes of this project – the transformation of a seventeenth century rural property – architect Bernard De Clerk invented a past history for the house. De Clerk imagined that the spacious single storey property had been increased in height to create another living floor; that the barn had been converted into a storeroom; and that, in around 1780, at the owners' request, the storeroom and house had been connected by a "recreational pavilion".

The architect's imaginary story was the starting point for the design of this building. The result integrates beautifully into the gardens that surround it. Construction company: Hyboma/Artebo.

The cleverness in this design is the way that modern interior design concepts have been adapted and incorporated into a more antiquated décor. The many built-in oak cupboards that can be seen in this feature perfectly complement the antique furniture.

P. 38-39
Two views of the living room. The oak cupboards blend into the panelling creating a refined and discrete effect.

P. 40-41
The informal kitchen and dining room with large unvarnished pitch pine cupboards and kitchen storage units made of painted wood.

P. 42-43
The library-cum-office in the attic of
the "recreational pavilion".

TRANSFORMATION

OF THE VILLA MARIE

Obumex was entrusted with the complete refurbishment of the Villa Marie and over the course of two years Kurt Neirynck (a senior interior architect at Obumex) completely transformed the property.

The classic cottage was renovated from top to bottom and significantly extended under the direction of architect Xavier Donck. The rooms were then redesigned in a contemporary style.

Kurt Neirynck created the interior design and coordinated its realisation in close collaboration with the owner. The personal touches make this character-filled house an enjoyable place to live. Whether recesses, hidden cupboards, a walk-in wardrobe, built-in cupboards or tailor-made bookcases, all of the storage spaces have been intelligently designed to facilitate day-to-day living.

P 44 and opposite
The living room is furnished with contemporary furniture. Glasses and crockery are stored in the painted cupboards built into the walls. The attention to detail is exceptional: the interior panels of these full height cupboards are made from the same wood as the television console table and the coffee table – so they even look attractive when they are open!
The paintings are by Dankers Décor.

P. 46-47
The light oak bookcase, designed by Axel Vervoordt, serves as the owner's office. It frames the settee and gives the room a warm and cosy atmosphere. An antique kilim from Azerbaijan and a collection of old legal works give the room an authentic quality. The antique desk is from the *Banque de France*.

The U-shaped kitchen with a central island is neatly delineated by the chalk-coloured cupboards, painted using a matt linseed oil paint, and the reclaimed bluestone countertop. Full length cupboards are preferred over wall cupboards above the work surfaces.

The enormous walk-in wardrobe leads into the master bedroom. Here the storage space is discreetly integrated into the headboard of the bed. The recess has become part of the décor itself.

THE MANY SIDES OF AN ANTIQUE

DEALER AND INTERIOR DESIGNER

A ntique dealer, Henri-Charles Hermans is a man of many talents. Over the years, this collector of curiosities has also specialised in the design and decoration of libraries, private office spaces and bespoke kitchens.

However, he has never forgotten his special connections with the antique world. For many years, he worked for an internationally renowned antique dealer and it was there that he developed a keen eye for beautiful furniture and precious artefacts from centuries gone by.

An English oak fireplace (from around 1820) flanked on both sides by a pair of modern bookcases with sliding shelves filled with nineteenth century artefacts.

This late nineteenth century cabinet is from northern France. The step-ladder is made from iron and wood.

This light oak cabinet (France, nineteenth century) has an impressively elegant design with its great height and minimal depth.

P. 52-53
The brand new bookcase was created in Polyèdre's English workshops. The dimensions of the light oak inlaid desk (from around 1860) are exceptional (250 x 220 cm).

MUTED AUSTERITY

his home in a former linen factory was designed by the architect Bernard De Clerk. The décor combines purity and simplicity with almost minimalist austerity.

The choice of materials accentuates the serenity of the house: Buxy Gris natural stone floors, grey French oak floorboards and, in the bedrooms, brushed veneer panelling and cupboards by Oregon. The homogenous tones and monochrome palette prevail throughout the house and reinforce the Zen atmosphere.

The kitchen, stairwell, bedroom and bathroom were designed by Marc Stellamans.

The pure, timeless design conceals a vast array of technical equipment including a floor heating and cooling system and an ingenious home technology system.

In the bedroom, Marc Stellamans has opted for a tinted, brushed wood by Oregon that creates an extremely calm and intimate atmosphere.

France Massangis stone was chosen for the bathroom. The wall panels and cupboards are made of brushed Oregon veneer.

Made-to-measure stainless steel handles.

Refined details: the switches and panels for the home technology system are made of stainless steel.

P. 56-57
The kitchen floor and countertop are made of Buxy Gris stone. The tailor-made cupboards are made of stained oak. Raffia chairs by Zanotta.

AN ANTIDOTE

TO A HECTIC LIFESTYLE

F ifteen years ago, Paul and Kaatje De Coster embarked on an adventurous project to transform an old windmill that had fallen into ruin into an antique shop and private home.

Their design is characterised, above all, by large, original furniture pieces (mostly in pitch pine or oak) and charming artefacts from times gone by.

These antique pieces are also functional and as such befit a twenty-first century interior. The simplicity of the timeless furniture serves as an antidote to modern life.

This bookcase measuring 5.10 m in length is from Ardennes. It dates from around 1900.

In this kitchen, as elsewhere in the house, the De Costers have chosen charming pieces that give their home a unique and timeless atmosphere.

A MONOCHROME PALETTE

This project reveals an unexpected side to interior designer Dominique Koch. Known until now for her romantic and colourful designs, she has decorated this holiday home in a simple style using a subtle monochrome selection of soothing white shades.

This bright and sunlight-filled house was inspired by the wooden houses of Long Island: same seaside holiday atmosphere, same simplicity, same gentle pace of life. All of the storage spaces in the house have a uniform design and merge discretely into the interior.

A view of the hallway on the first floor. Here, as elsewhere, tall panels conceal practical storage spaces.

The bathtub and washbasin are made of a natural sand-coloured stone called Jerusalem stone. The colours of the blinds also evoke the nearby beach.

The various living rooms are separated by sliding doors. These make it possible to create a more intimate atmosphere in a house where a sense of space and openness prevails. A photograph by Muriel Emsens hangs above two poufs covered in grey kaki linen. The oak table was designed specifically for this house by Dominique Koch.

The meticulous use of high-quality natural materials – double fleece-lined white linen curtains, untreated oak floors etc. – creates an air of simple refinement. This south-facing living room looks out onto a magnificent garden. The room is flooded with light.

The oak table is Dominique Koch's own creation. The chairs are covered in a washable "Dune" coloured fabric from Bruder. The artwork is by Georges Van Rijk.

RESTORATION OF A BEAUTIFUL

1930S APPARTMENT

Interior architect Vanessa De Meulder lives in a beautiful apartment building dating back to 1926.

She has completely redesigned the apartment rooms to fulfil her own requirements, while at the same time respecting the period elements and proportions.

The dark walls and cupboards create an intimate atmosphere. Soft, subtle lighting by Christian Liaigre. The metal table and chair are from the period. The stripes on the carpet accentuate the depth of the room. The mirror doors make this small room appear visibly larger.

The original "Cubex" kitchen is typical of the period. It has been given a new look with new soft bluestone work surfaces, brushed stainless steel doors and a stained parquet floor. The top cupboards are accessed using the suspended ladder. "Hello" chairs from Artifort.

A PEACEFUL AND

SPACIOUS HOME IN CAMPINE

I n this feature, interior architect Monique Heeren presents two rooms from her own house in Campine.

This project began in a somewhat unusual manner, since Heeren first designed the interior spaces and only then sought out an architect to design the exterior. Using this method, she was able to create a layout which makes optimum use of the available space. Her choice of décor is classic and elegant.

The library is decorated entirely in bleached oak panelling, complemented by a burgundy linen blind and an antique armchair re-covered in a Mulberry check wool fabric. Busts (late nineteenth–early twentieth century) by the sculptor Pierre-Henri Van Perck feature throughout the house.

The floor of the orangery is laid with reclaimed flagstones from Burgundy in a wide range of pastel shades. The linen curtains are edged with a border to break up the impression of height. The walls have been coated using a lime-based plaster and coloured using pigments that match the curtains.

A DELIGHTFUL RENOVATION

OF A SEMI-DETACHED HOUSE

nterior architect Nathalie Van Reeth has transformed this typical semi-detached house from the beginning of the last century into a pleasant and contemporary living space.

Her aim was to open up the rooms and let more light in, since the traditional layout, consisting of a row of rooms and a central stairwell, made the middle room very cramped. The result is an airy, well-organised and contemporary space. The white versus dark wood contrast is found throughout the property and gives the design an elegant, minimalist touch.

The central room has been turned into a library. The shelves with invisible fixtures give a lighter feel to the ensemble. The mouldings, parquet floor and old bevelled glass door have been preserved and lovingly restored.

An elegant and original headboard: the wall behind the bed serves as a bookcase and light stand. The bed is made of oak stained in the same colour.
The bedroom leads into the walk-in wardrobe and bathroom giving the impression that you are in a suite.

The rooms at the back of the house have been opened out to create a large space with a raised terrace. Light floods into the space through the large tailor-made metal window. The kitchen units are made of painted MDF; the worktops have been stained in a darker shade. The floor has been finished with white epoxy. The wenge table is tailor-made. The floor has been stained in the same dark colour.

REFINEMENT IN THE COUNTRYSIDE

This large, charming eighteenth century house is surrounded by English-style gardens, designed by the mistress of the house, which adjoin both a kitchen and flower garden. Behind the property an enchanting pavilion, river and hundred-year-old trees further enhance with beauty of the grounds.

The master of the house loves large open spaces, beautiful materials and antique furniture. The mistress is the epitome of English country charm and can often be seen walking through the grounds in a pair of boots, secateurs in hand and followed by her many dogs, constantly trimming and pruning her favourite plants.

Once architect Antoine de Radigues had extended the original building and beautifully restored the entire property, the owners asked Christine Lemaitre and Amélie de Borchgrave (Chintz Shop) to help them choose the colours, curtains and fabrics for their home. The ensemble has a classic, elegant and extremely cosy character.

A large kitchen-cum-dining room where friends and family can get together in a rather unconventional setting. The ultra professional, yet warm, kitchen was designed with the master of the house – an experienced cook and lover of fine foods – in mind. All sides offer a view over the grounds and kitchen garden.

Another view of the kitchen showing the dining area with its large antique bookcase for storing cookery and gardening books. The curtains made from faded ticking fabric (Chintz Shop) hang from a large mahogany stained wood curtain pole. The floor is made of sandstone.

A pair of paintings by Thierry Bosquet. An old stripped-down door and, on the ceiling, a large Venetian lantern.

The small lounge for the mistress of the house. The walls have been painted English green. The meridienne has been re-covered in an old faded chintz.

Toile de Jouy print curtains and paintings of flowers and gardens.

A NEW LEASE OF LIFE

T his house, which was built in 1958 by the architect Viérin in an idyllic setting close to a golf course, has recently been transformed by interior architect Philip Simoen.

From the outside, this classic villa remains unchanged. However, the interior has been given a completely new lease of life: the new design combines stylish contemporary furniture from the collections of Christian Liaigre, Le Corbusier, Maarten Van Severen and more with exclusive bespoke pieces made from sycamore and pear tree wood.

Today, a sense of class and discrete luxury abounds throughout the house. Simoen's choice of warm, durable materials combined with his penchant for purity has created a simple and serene space. The angular-shaped storage units are key elements of the décor.

P. 76-77

The lounge, complete with fireplace, was created by De Puydt.
To the left of the fireplace is a tailor-made hi-fi cabinet; to the right is a cupboard concealing a plasma screen. The coffee table is also tailor-made. The armchair and settee are by Christian Liaigre. The cotton, silk and linen rug is by Bartholomeus.

The bespoke cupboards are made of pear tree wood. Le Corbusier furniture created for Cassina.

View of the library from the hall.
A silkscreen print of Lenin by
Andy Warhol.

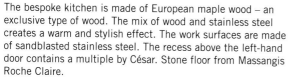

The bespoke kitchen is made of European maple wood – an exclusive type of wood. The mix of wood and stainless steel creates a warm and stylish effect. The work surfaces are made of sandblasted stainless steel. The recess above the left-hand door contains a multiple by César. Stone floor from Massangis Roche Claire.

This sycamore walk-in wardrobe has been made entirely to measure. The central set of drawers doubles as a folding table. In-built lighting by Modular and bench by Christian Liaigre.

A PHENOMENAL COUNTRY HOUSE

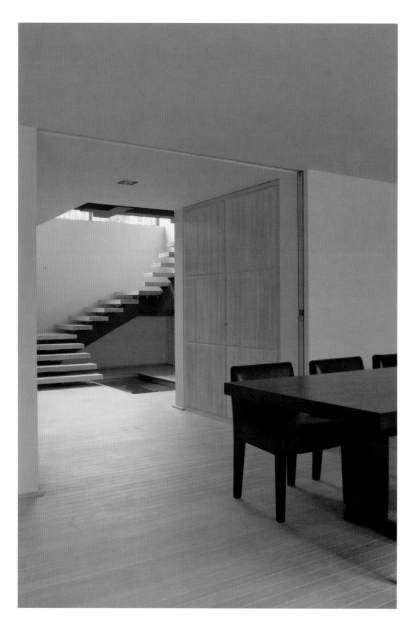

This house, designed by the architect Librecht in 1970, has been transformed by its current owners: a couple with three children.

Architecture firm Instore was given carte blanche when it came to creating an interior design for the whole of this exceptional country property. Its aim: to create a contemporary space in a minimalist style softened by the widespread use of warm natural materials such as wood. The opening up of the space and the creation of angles were also key aspects of the design. The use of homogeneous materials and colours makes for a pure, serene atmosphere. The entire space has the feel of a loft conversion: you are free to move around and the spaces are generous and open.

Every element of the design has been thoroughly thought through and designed especially for this exclusive home, from the handles on the doors and furniture, to the bathroom accessories, to the tailor-made furniture. The entire property has been equipped with a highly sophisticated home technology system.

The floorboards and all of the bespoke oak furniture have been stained grey.

P. 82-83
The creation of angles and a sense of space were fundamental to this project by the company Instore. The rooms contain very little furniture, which reinforces the sense of an abnormal abundance of space.

P. 84-85
An ultra stylish, contemporary kitchen equipped with a Viking kitchen range. Chairs by Flexform (Mixer model).

P. 86-87
The design for this bathroom again makes use of raw materials, creating a natural and contemporary atmosphere. The bathtub, washbasins and taps are from Boffi.

A PASSION FOR CRAFTSMANSHIP

Francis Van Damme trained as a lawyer, but his eye for aesthetics and his love of authentic hand-made materials has been growing since his childhood.

In 1995, his dream became a reality. Along with a team of passionate craftspeople, Van Damme founded an artisan carpentry workshop making beautiful panelling, bespoke furniture pieces, bookcases and more, exclusively from reclaimed materials and antique items. His attention to detail and desire for perfection are evident in all of his unique restoration projects that restore time-worn materials to grandeur.

P. 88-89
These two wardrobes were created by Francis Van Damme's artisan carpentry workshop.

WHEN KITCHEN

AND LOUNGE COMBINE

A rchitecture firm Themenos designs projects in a diverse range of styles, be it classic or minimalist, timeless or rural, English Cotswold or Tudor, modern or spacious.

It designs its kitchens with passionate amateur cooks in mind. For these lovers of fine foods, this room occupies a central place in their lives and they generally have high expectations. The owner of this tranquil kitchen wanted a kitchen fitted with semi-professional equipment. However the main factor in his final choice of kitchen was his emotional connection to this room and his desire to feel at home while he is cooking.

The subtle, indirect light from the dresser enhances the friendly atmosphere around the authentic monastery table.

P. 91-93

The functions of the kitchen and living room are combined in this kitchen.
Only the enormous fireplace still evokes the atmosphere of an authentic stately home kitchen.
The La Cornue kitchen range (photograph 92-93) occupies a central position. The reclaimed
bluestone Burgundy flagstones perfectly complement the olive and silver colours of the walls.

P. 94-95
Classic proportions and the use of age-old construction techniques: Themenos'
designs are simplicity itself and make use of majestic materials that improve with
age.

LIVING AND WORKING

IN SERENE SURROUNDINGS

The kitchen and dining room are combined. From here you can enjoy a superb view over the swimming pool in the new internal courtyard.

T he designer of this house belonging to the architect Pascal Van Der Kelen received international recognition when he created this home in 1994.

In 2005 the architect transformed this house-cum-studio, adding an extra wing to house the lounge in order to create more space for his office that is now located in the old living room.

An enormous bookcase has been suspended above the lower window. In the background is the internal courtyard and swimming pool.

A MODERN FEEL

TO A CLASSIC VILLA

T he owners of this classic villa in the green suburbs of Brussels appointed the design firm Instore to fit out their bathroom and library.

Ultimately, however, the entire house was transformed, with many of the traditional design features – typical of a French style villa from this period – being removed in order to create greater space and clean proportions.

A Casamilano console table stands in the hallway. The wood panelled flooring is made of stained oak. The stained oak walls in the back-left corner of the picture conceal large storage spaces.

P 99-101
The monochrome palette, warm materials and simple shapes give the new interior an air of calmness and serenity. The oak panelling has been sanded down and lightly stained. Flexform settees (Bob model) surround a table by Maxalto. The rug is by Paola Lenti and the spotlights are by Modular.

The same sanded, stained oak is used for the cupboards in the bedroom.

P. 102
The sanded, stained oak woodwork was designed specifically for this house by Instore. This material and finish are found throughout the house. The work surface and table top are made of Basaltina lava stone.
The dining room chairs were created for Emeco by Philippe Starck.

The shower and the wall above the bathtub are decorated with a Moma marble mosaic.

The use of sanded, stained oak in the bedroom and walk-in wardrobe creates a harmonious atmosphere. MDF bed by Lim.

White marble washbasin and bathtub by Carrare. Taps by Boffi.

RESTORATION OF AN EIGHTEENTH

CENTURY APARTMENT

This apartment is housed in a historic building that was recently renovated in its entirety.

The brief given by the owners to interior architect Annick Colle was to create a space that would evoke the eighteenth century in all its splendour.

The apartment also had to fulfil two other functions: it had to serve both as an intimate home and as an exclusive space for receiving visitors.

P. 106-107
The poplar wood panelling was created for a hunting pavilion for Louis XVI (1780) at the Château de Deulin, which is now the home of Stéphane de Harlez. Finish created by Dankers Décor.
The folding shutters in the panelling conceal a kitchenette (P. Vancronenburg).

P. 108-109
The master bedroom with a view over the secret internal garden.
The original black gloss finish on the Chinese console table (late eighteenth century) has been preserved (Philippe Farahnick gallery).

CLEAN LINES IN A RURAL SETTING

I n this feature, interior architect Alexis Herbosch, the founder and inspiration behind Apluz, presents his pure design for a country home.

The dominant features of the design are the interaction between the rooms and the views over the garden from the house's many windows. In-built storage spaces can be found throughout the house. These are all concealed behind poplar wood panels, which give the interior a distinctive homogeneous appearance.

Apluz can create designs to delight any owner. In every one of its interior design projects – whether it be the renovation of an English cottage, a long, narrow farmhouse in Campine, a modern loft conversion or an eighteenth century aristocrat's house – Apluz turns its clients' ideas and wishes into reality.

The wall behind the gas kitchen range is made of black zelliges, which contrast starkly with the poplar panels on the kitchen wall. The island has been placed in a central position, so that the owners can look out onto the garden while they cook. The countertop is made of soft bluestone.

The poplar wood panels create a serene atmosphere in the entrance hall.
The door to the cellar – complete with an opening that serves as a cat flap – is concealed.
Large loosely-laid soft bluestone tiles were chosen for the floor.
A narrow service door with peephole provides secret access to the kitchen.
The sliding door in the living area can be used to close off the open-plan rooms and create a more intimate atmosphere to complement the open fireplace.

P. 112-113

The bench to the left of the open fireplace (with poplar wood surround) offers a view over the garden.

The open shelves on the right house old books and antiques.

Items from the owner's antique collection are displayed on the old folding market table behind the settee.

The floor lamp (by Aluminate) next to the settee was designed by Apluz and comprises a solid oak base and a cloth lampshade.

The existing pine floorboards were salvaged and treated to give them the appearance of being time-worn.

In all the rooms, ceiling height natural linen blinds accentuate the height of the space.

A SENSE OF SPACE

he interior of this magnificent apartment, complete with garden and terrace and measuring more than 500 m², was designed by Nathalie Delabye of Ensemble & Associés and furnished by Isabelle Reynders using only Christian Liaigre pieces.

Working in close collaboration with their client, the designers, both of whom have a penchant for quasi invisible details, have created an apartment in which a pure and simple design creates a sense of well-being. The austere chic style prevails throughout the apartment.

P. 114 and opposite
The bookcase, shelves and all of the
woodwork are made of sanded,
bleached oak. The vine black linen
Basile armchairs are by Christian
Liaigre, as are the white leather Autan
daybed and Openwork pedestal table.

View of the kitchen designed by Ensemble & Associés and created by Obumex. The
countertop and central island are made of reconstituted stone from Unistone and
the cupboards are made of sanded, bleached oak. The cooker hood has been tailor-
made using stadip glass and brushed stainless steel. Stools by Claire Bataille.

The master bedroom and wardrobe were designed and created exclusively for this apartment using sanded, bleached oak. The room leads through to the bathroom and cinema room.

The guest bathroom is fitted with a bespoke washbasin made of reconstituted stone from Unistone and a unit made of sanded, bleached oak.
The taps are by Dornbracht. The main bathroom is made of varnished reconstituted stone from Unistone.

HOME SERIES

Volume 15 : STORAGE SPACE

The reports in this book are selected from the Beta-Plus collection of home-design books: www.betaplus.com
They have been compiled in a special series by Le Figaro in French language: Ma Déco

Copyright © 2009 Beta-Plus Publishing / Le Figaro
Originally published in French language

PUBLISHER
Beta-Plus Publishing
Termuninck 3
B – 7850 Enghien
Belgium
www.betaplus.com
info@betaplus.com

TEXT
Alexandra Druesne

PHOTOGRAPHY
Jo Pauwels

DESIGN
Polydem - Nathalie Binart

TRANSLATIONS
Txt-Ibis

ISBN : 978-90-8944-046-4

Printed in China

P. 120-121
A Marie-Rêve design. The back wall is composed entirely of tinted oak panels. The floor has been re-laid using reclaimed oak railway carriage panelling. The curtains are made of painted linen.

P. 122-123
A project by Stéphanie Laporte. The old oak and wenge floor with its superb marquetry has been finished with a clear varnish. Contemporary furniture by Maxalto. Work of art entitled Partial Truth by Bruce Nauman. The storage space is very discreetly hidden away behind the panelling.

P. 124-125
A Philip Simoen creation.

P. 126-127
A kitchen designed by Sphere Concepts.